Convent Belles

created by

☆ margaret **CARROLL**

☆ jerry **McCUE**

art by

☆ al **KILGORE, jr.**

ABOUT COMICS | CAMARILLO, CALIFORNIA

Convent Belles
Originally published by A. A. Hadinger, 1952
About Comics edition published July, 2018

The characters in this book never appeared in print before. They were created by Margaret Carroll and Jerry McCue for use in a series of cartoon books of which this is the first. Any similarity to person living or dead is purely coincidental.

Customized editions available

Send all queries to *questions@aboutcomics.com*

The Characters
APPEARING IN THIS BOOK

SISTER BERNADETTE
SISTER CECILIA
MOTHER ANGELICA ....*the Mother Superior*
MONSIGNOR O'MALLEY......................*the Rector*
FATHER FLYNN.........................*the Parish Priest*
ROCCO AND RILEY.......*the Twin-Spirits of class-room life*
OLIVER...............................*the Boy Intellectual*
O'FLAHERTY..............................*the Gardener*
MRS. O'LEARY....................*the Rectory Housekeeper*
MULLIGAN...............................*the Policeman*
MR. CLANCY..........................*the Truant-Officer*

The Originators
MARGARET CARROLL *and* JERRY McCUE
are the Creators of the Characters, Gags and Situations
appearing in this book

The Staff

AL KILGORE, JR...............................*Artwork*
ROBERT HOOD ST. CYR .... *Ecclesiastical Research*
GIAN FILIPPO CIARA-MELLE ....*Technical Advisor*
OSCAR HALSTED ....*Compilation*
HUGH MONTGOMERY.......................*Production*
J. FOSTER GIBBS ....*Publicity*

"M-M-M-M-M-M-M"

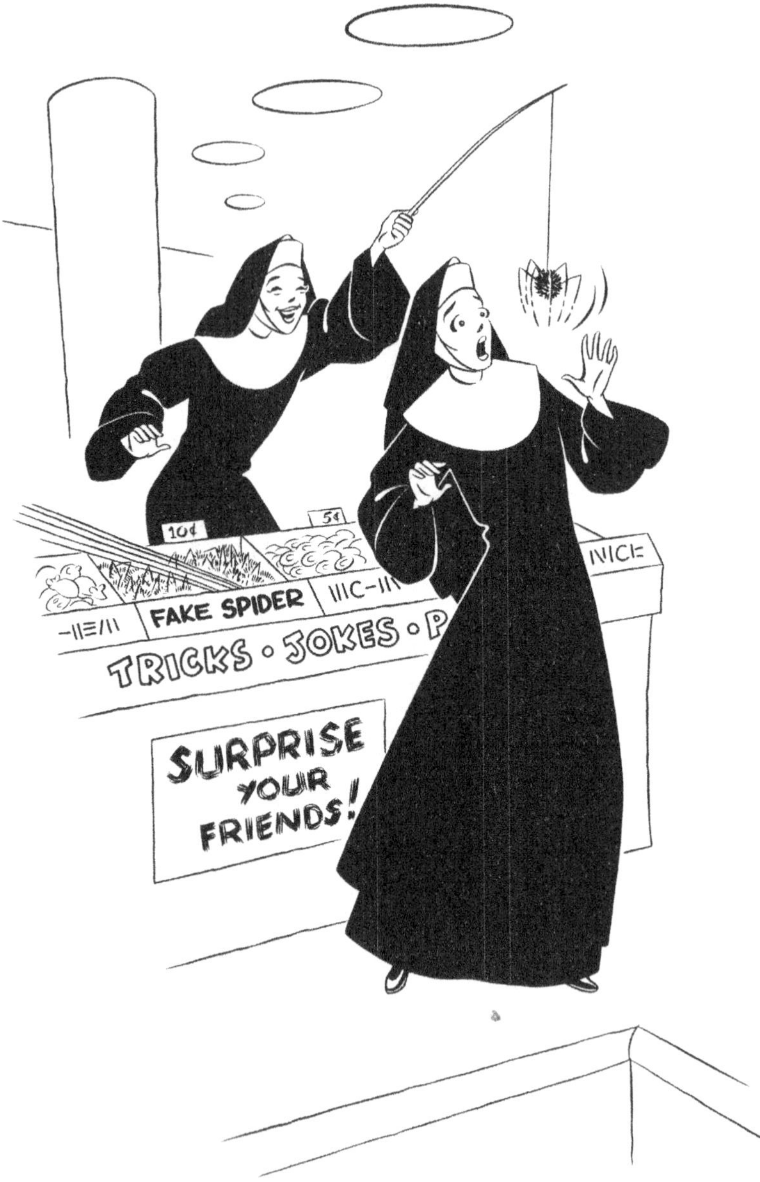
10¢
5¢
FAKE SPIDER
TRICKS • JOKES • P
SURPRISE
YOUR
FRIENDS!

"I LIKE THIS STORE 'CAUSE IT'S A LONGER RIDE"

"I NEVER DID LIKE BANANAS!"

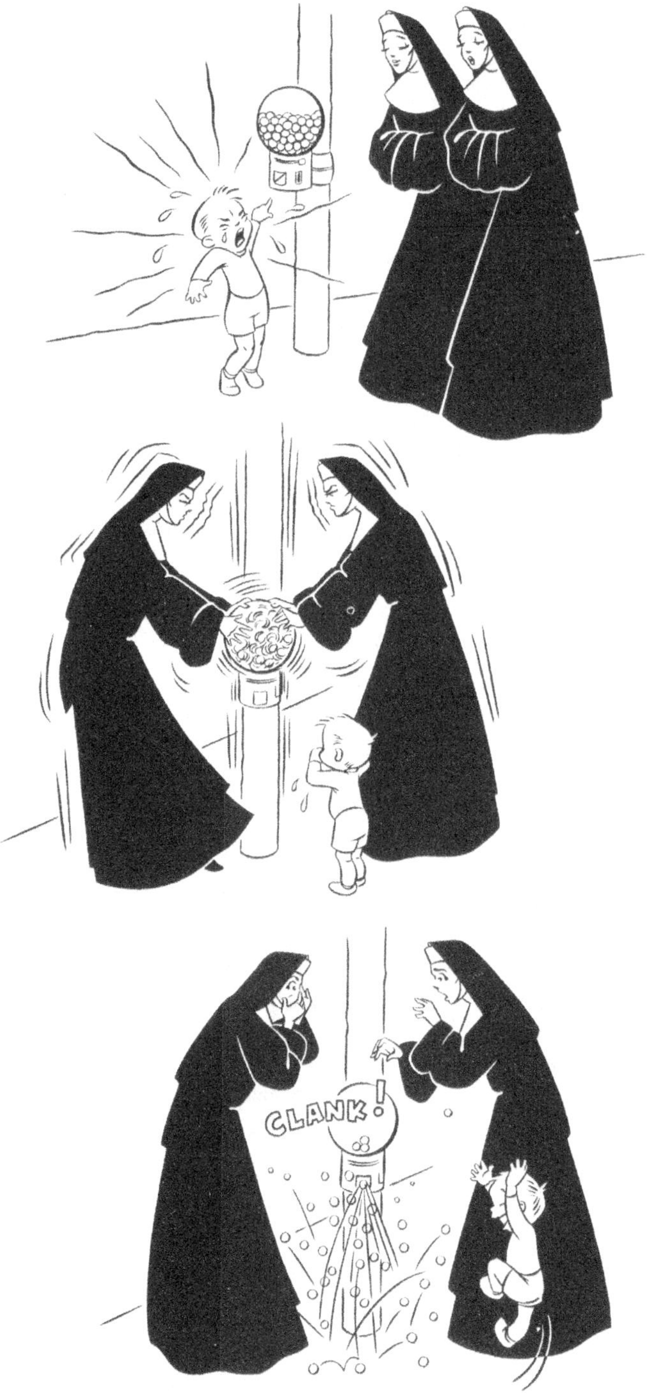
CLANK!

"I USED TO BACK HOME"

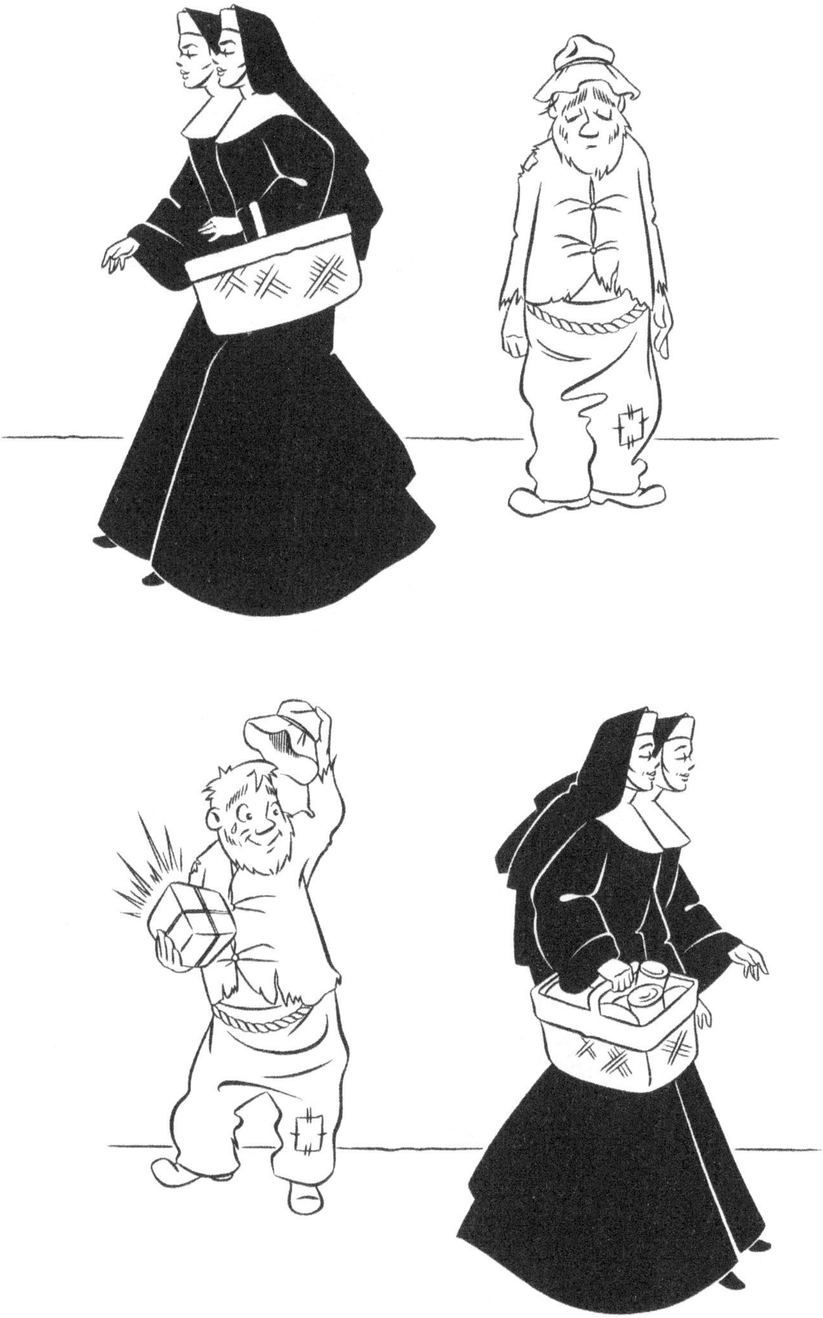

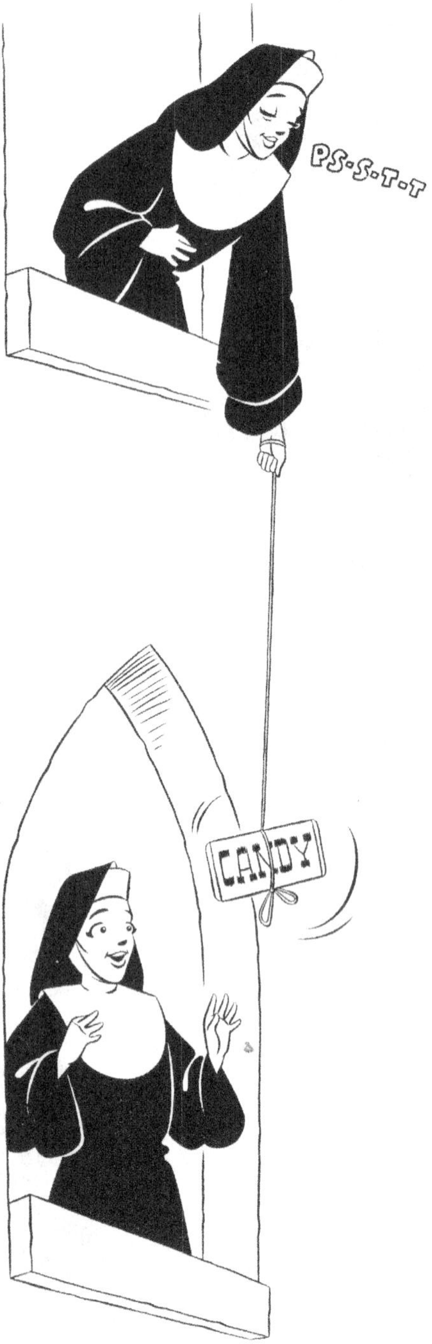
PS-S-T-T
CANDY

"LET'S, JUST ONCE"

"THIS, I'VE GOT TO SEE!"

"BELIEVE IT OR NOT, PARDNER — WE'RE LOST!"

"WELL, HOW DID HOPPETY MAKE OUT?"

"YOU'RE NEXT"

"NOT OXYGEN, SOMEBODY SNUCK HIM AN ONION SANDWICH!"

- "SOME PEANUTS FOR THE MONKEYS, PLEASE"
- "HOW MAN'A-YOU GOT?"

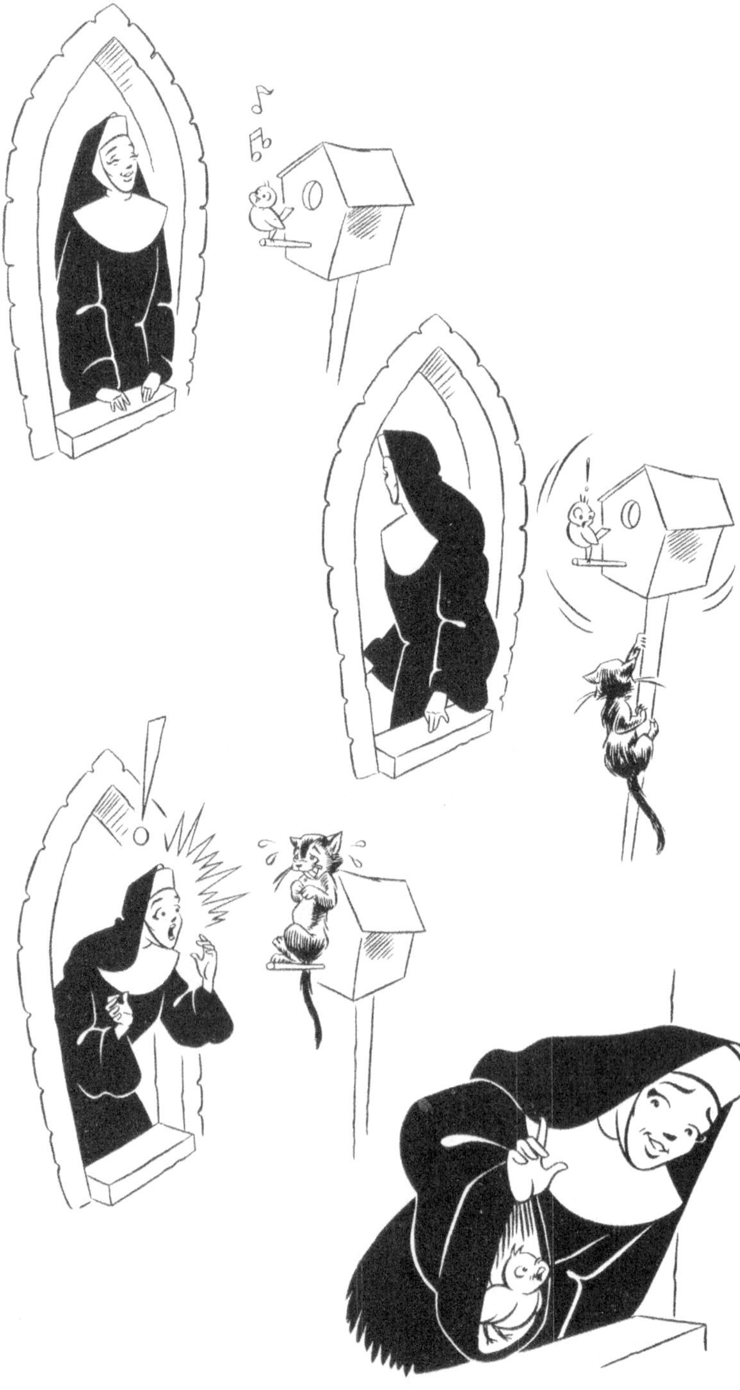

"STEPHEN FOSTER OR NO STEPHEN FOSTER—
THIS HORRIBLE NOISE HAS GOT TO STOP!"

"AH! SPRING IS REALLY HERE"

"O'FLAHERTY HAS COMPANY FOR DINNER"

"MAYBE O'FLAHERTY IS DOWN WITH A COLD, BUT I REMEMBER LAST ST. PATRICK'S DAY"

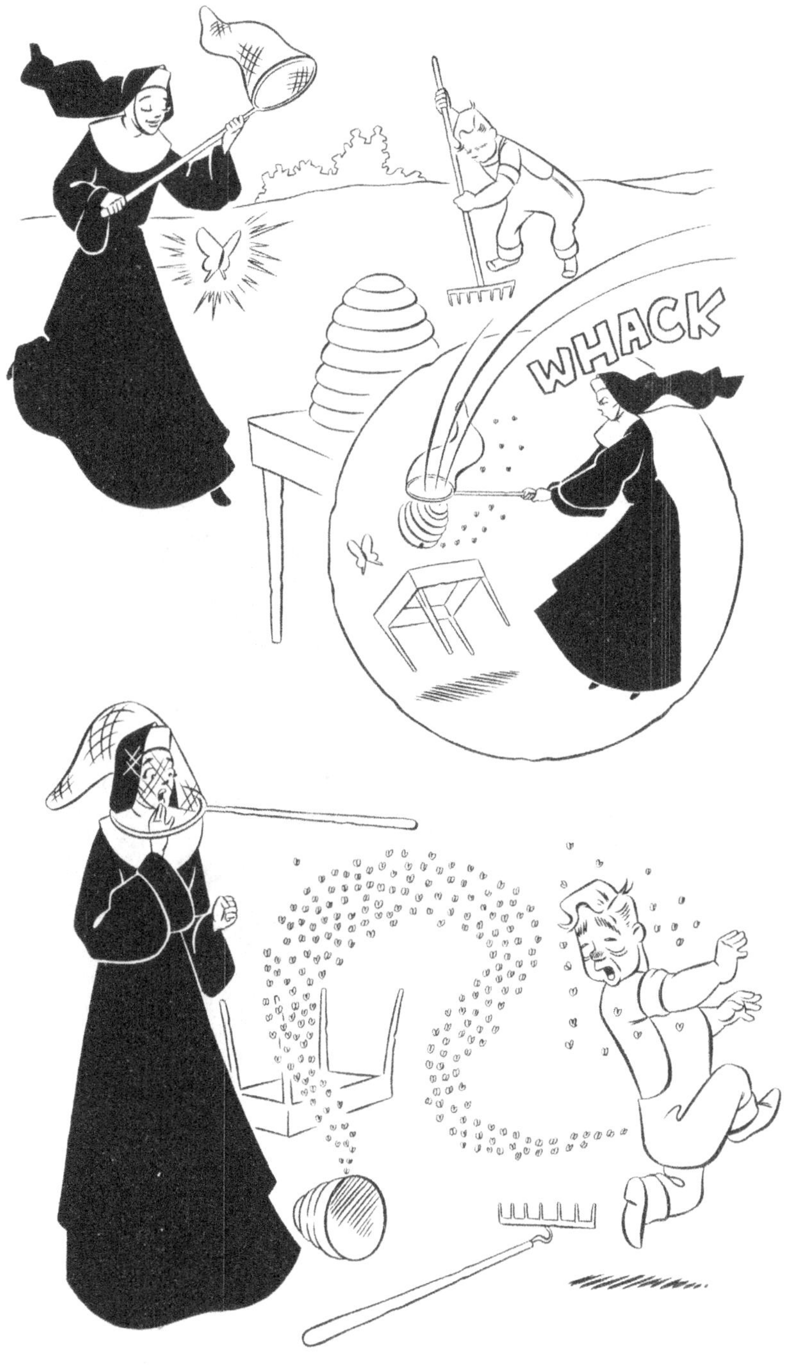
WHACK

"IS IT NECESSARY TO GROW SO MUCH SPINACH?"

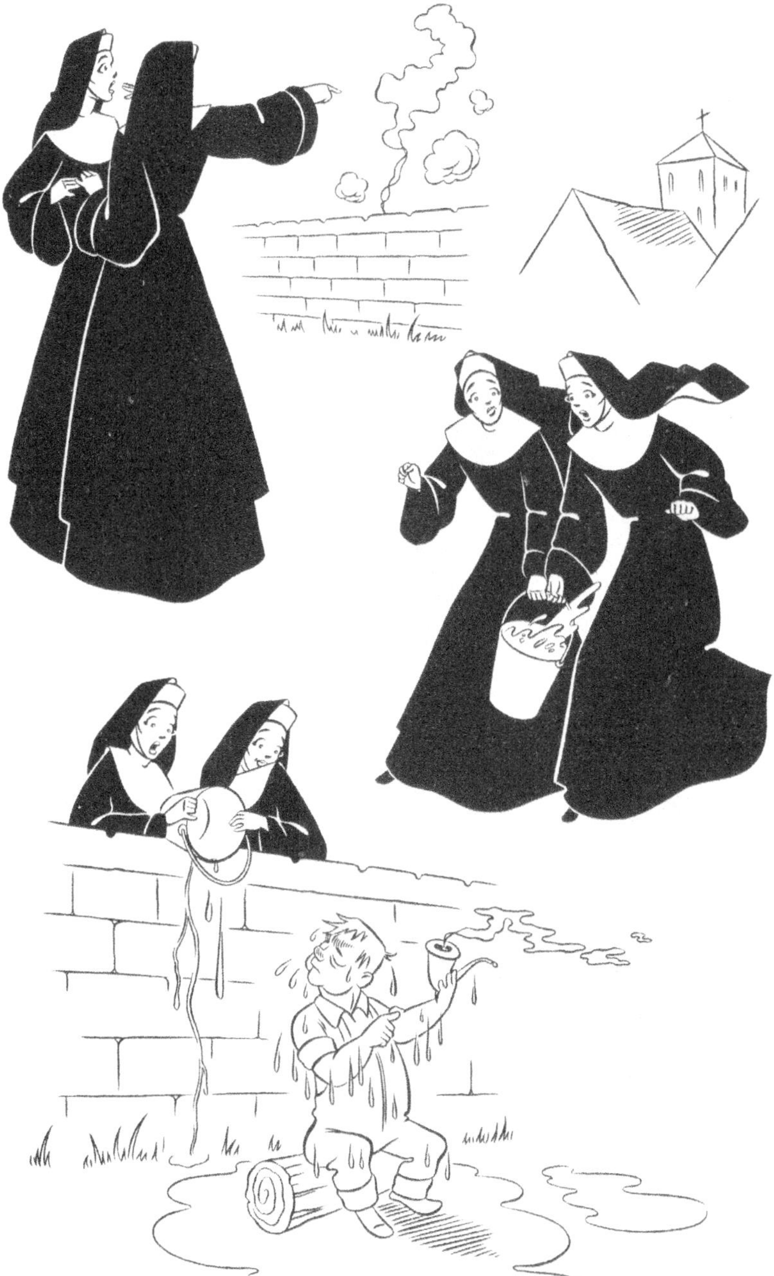

"NOW CAN YOU STOP IT?"

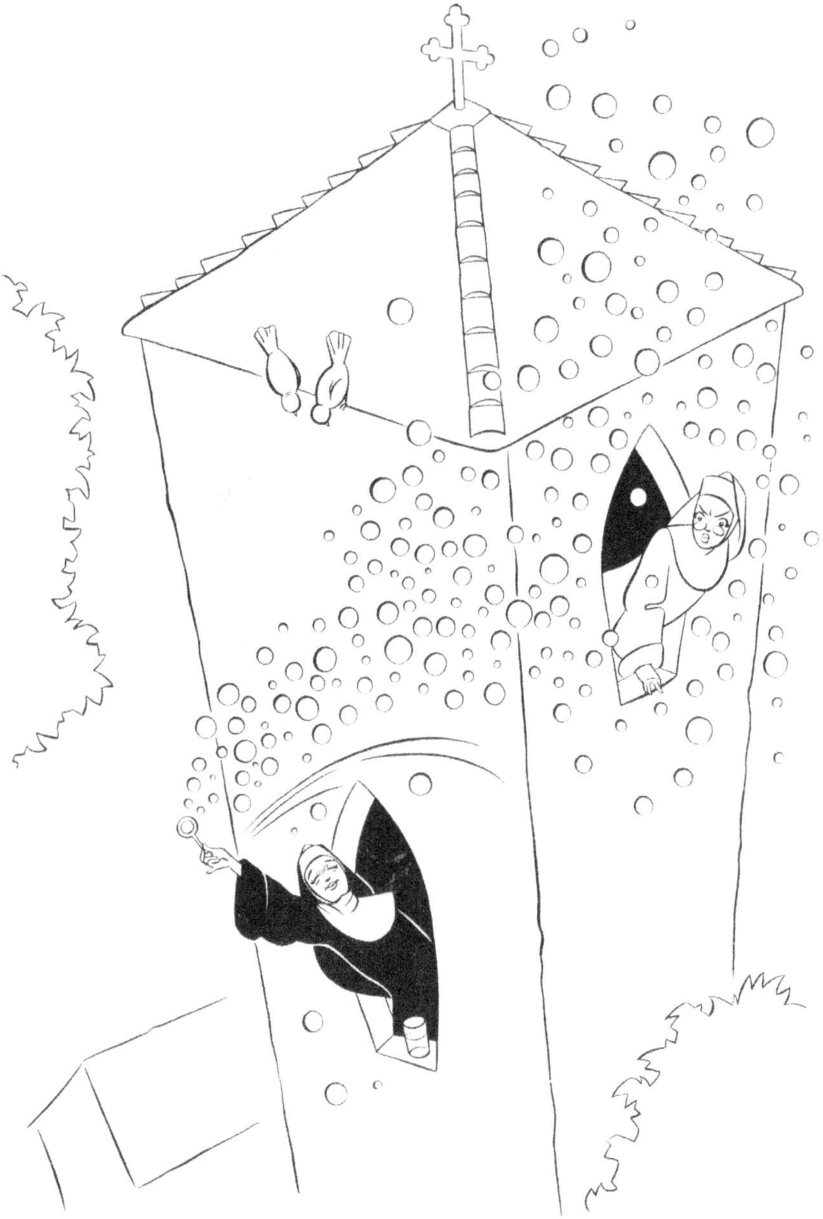

"BUT, WHAT'LL WE DO WITH THEM ALL?"

"WONDER WHY IT STOPPED"

"RILEY!"

"YOU DROPPED YOUR SHOULDER — THAT'S WHY YOU CAUGHT IT!"

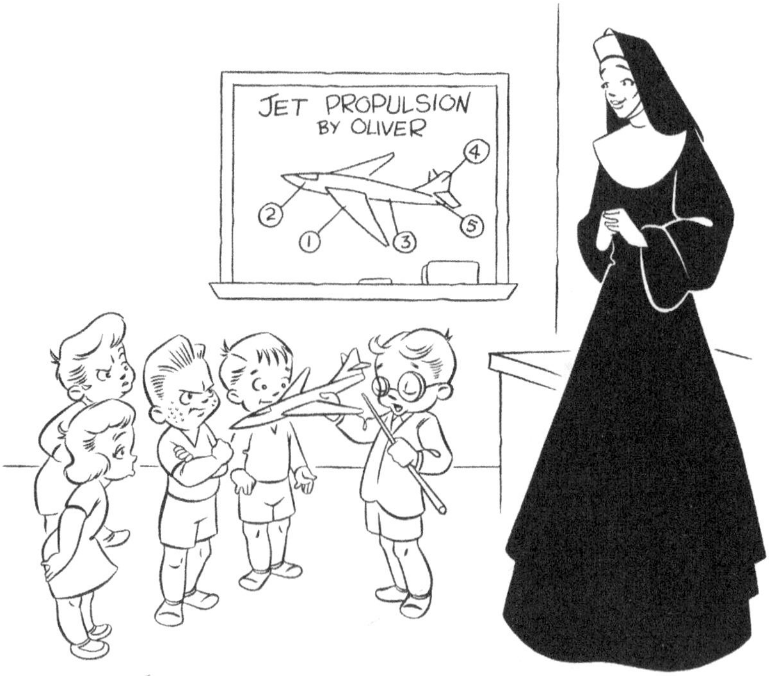
JET PROPULSION
BY OLIVER
1
2
3
4
5

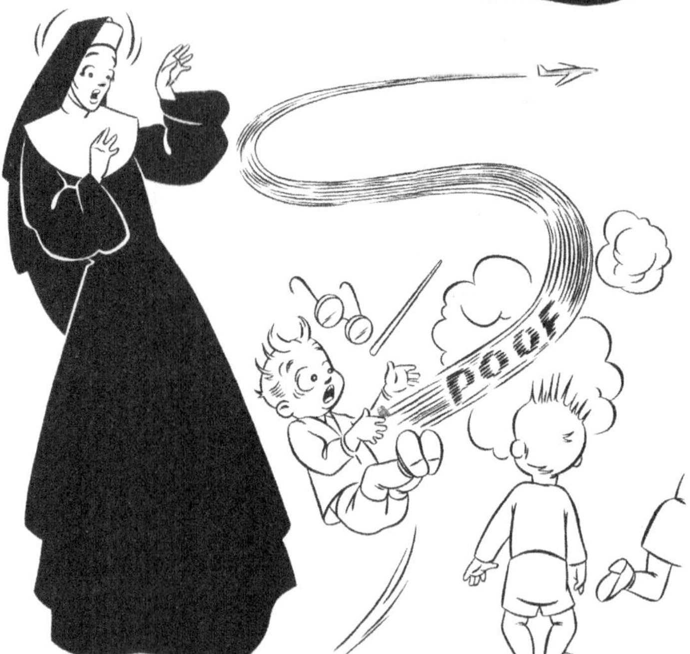
POOF

- "IF THIS DOESN'T GO OFF, WE'RE STUCK"
- "AND IF IT DOES GO OFF, YOU'RE REALLY STUCK!"

"OKAY EINSTEIN - EVERYTIME ONE OF US GETS OFF, YOU SUBTRACT - GET IT?"

- "STOP WORRYIN' THAT'S ONLY THE FROGS' CROAKIN'"
- "YEAH, BUT IT SOUNDS LIKE CLANCY, THE TRUANT OFFICER, AND IT GIVES ME THE WILLIES!"

"YOU PUSH ME, THEN I'LL PUSH YOU"

"WHADDA YA CALL THAT?"

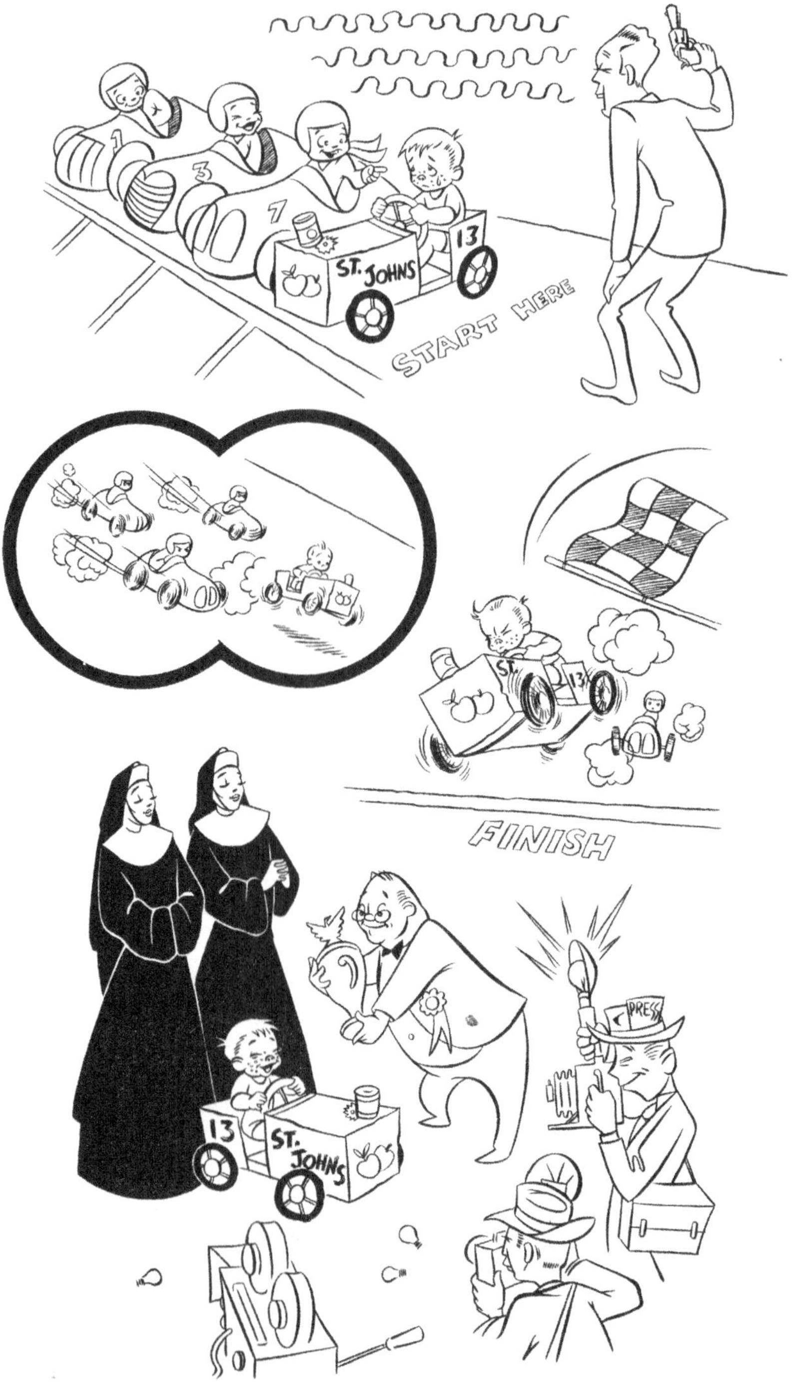
1
3
7
13
ST. JOHNS
START HERE
ST.
13
FINISH
PRESS
13
ST. JOHNS

"PICKIN' VIOLETS — THAT SETTLES IT!"

"WHAT NEXT THROUGH THESE PORTALS?"

"THEY'RE TO KEEP THE SAND OUTA YER SHOES, — I GUESS!"

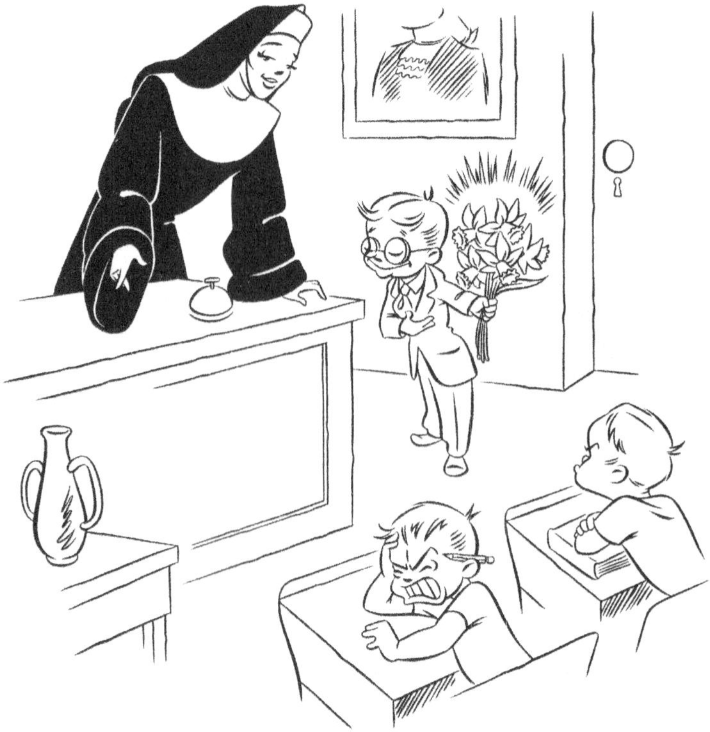

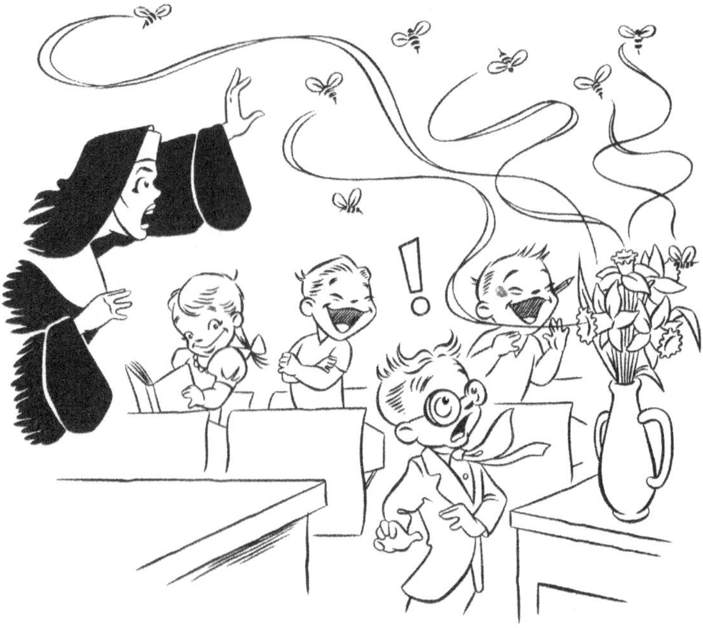

"WE BROUGHT THE TOTS IN, LIKE YOU SAID, MR. SPIELHEIMER"

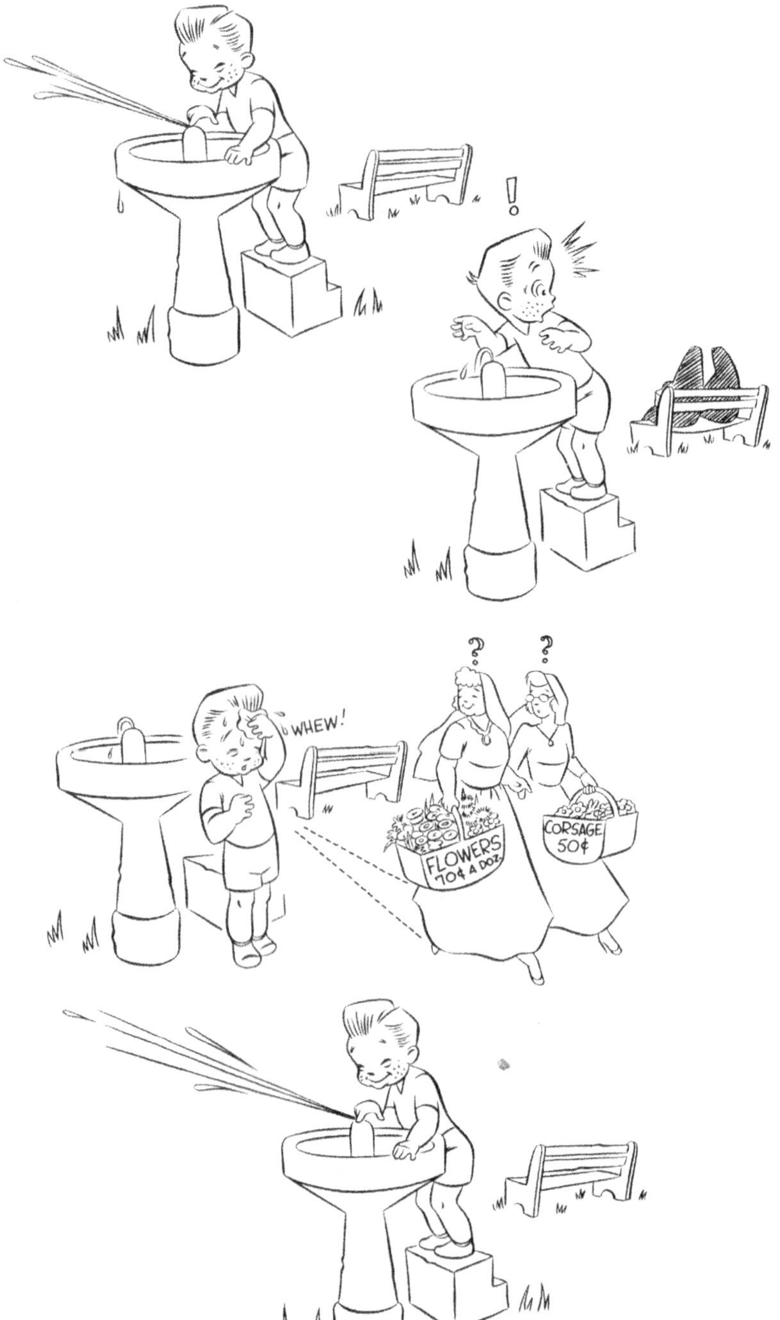
!
WHEW!
?
?
FLOWERS 70¢ A DOZ.
CORSAGE 50¢

"SHALL WE?"

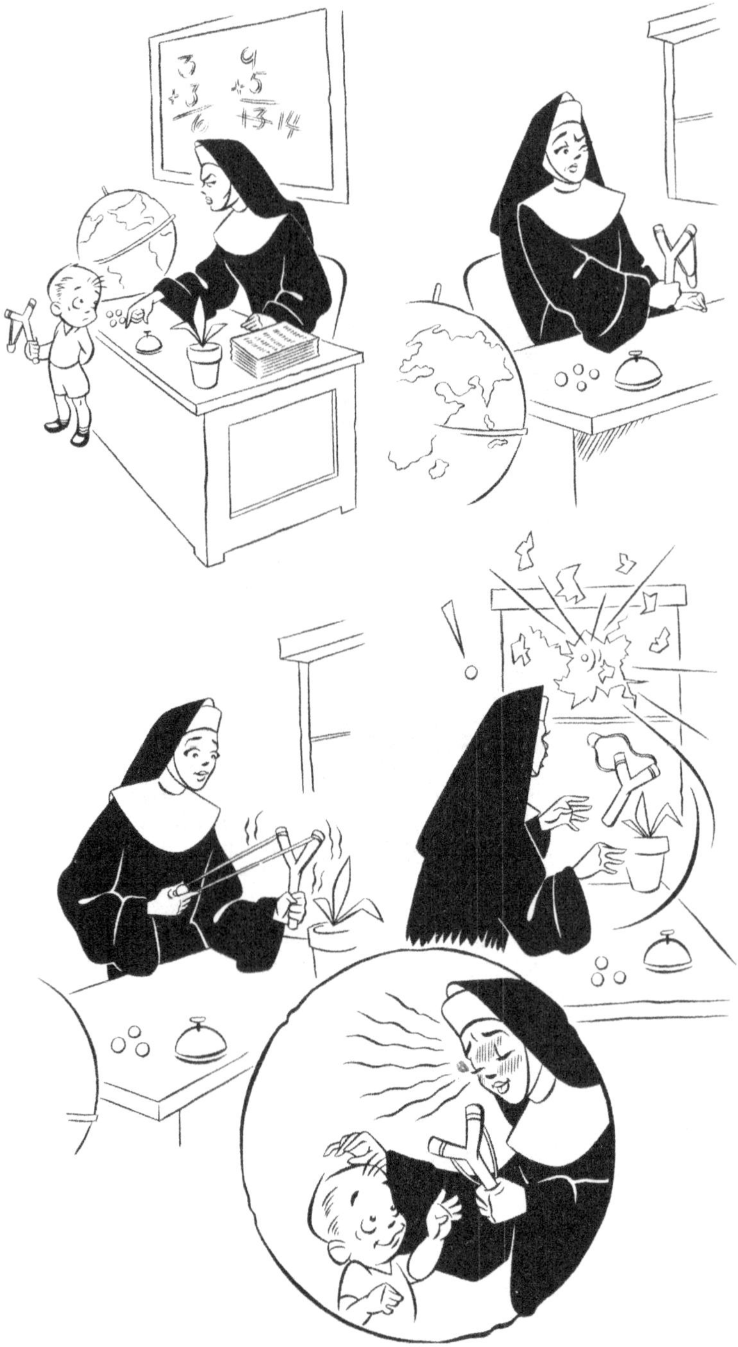

THE AD-LIB

"THE WALTZ IS ONE-TWO-THREE, ONE-TWO-THREE, LIKE THIS!"

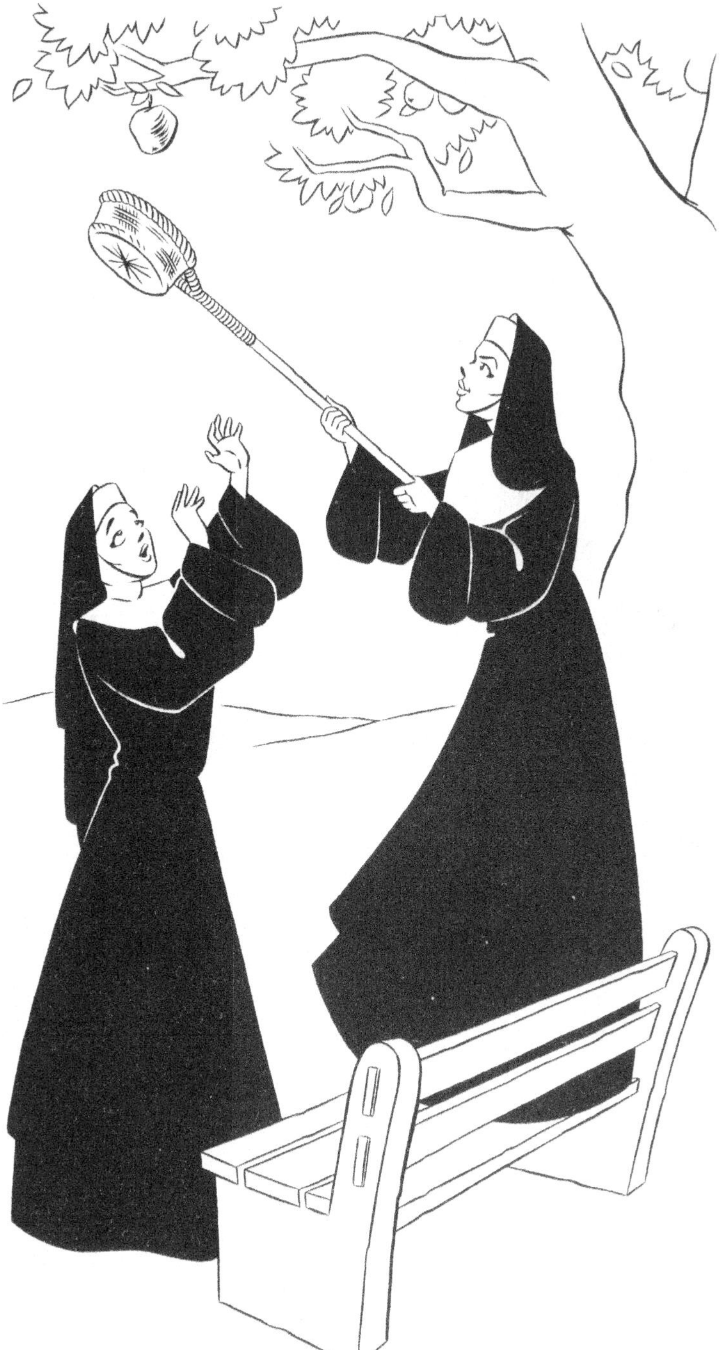

"WHO SAID 3 TEASPOONSFUL TO 1 CUP — IT'S 1 TEASPOONFUL TO 3 CUPS!!!"

º "YOUR PINKY FINGER ISN'T TOUCHING THE KEYS, AT ALL!"
º "IT'S SHORTER THAN THE OTHERS, THAT'S WHY!"

"I FOUND SOME YARN UNDER MY DESK"

"THAR SHE BLOWS, SISTER"

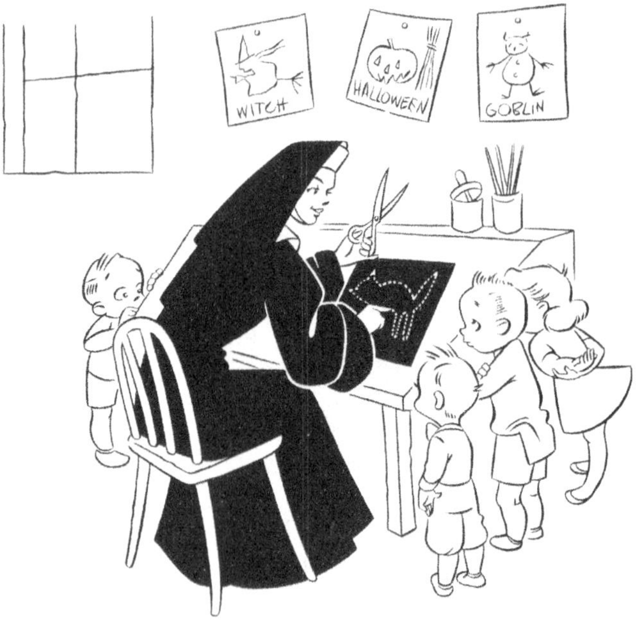
WITCH
HALLOWEEN
GOBLIN

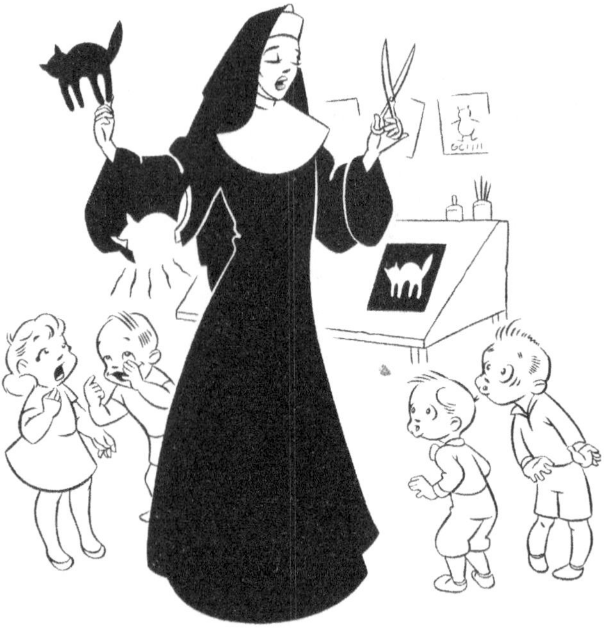

WILLIAM TELL • ANTI-CLIMAX

"THEN WE'LL TALK TO THE MANAGER, ALL THESE CHILDREN ARE 7 OR UNDER, AND WE ARE ADULTS, FOR SURE!!"

"NO BRASS RINGS, GOVERNMENT PRIORITY, SISTER"

"IT WAS FATHER FLYNNS' IDEA TO SHOW US A NEW PLAY"

- "NOW WHO'S GOING TO DIG US OUT?"
- "GUESS WHO?"

"HOW THAT MAN LOVES THAT HORN!"

"IT'S NOT THE ORGAN — SOMEONE'S VOICE IS CHANGING!"

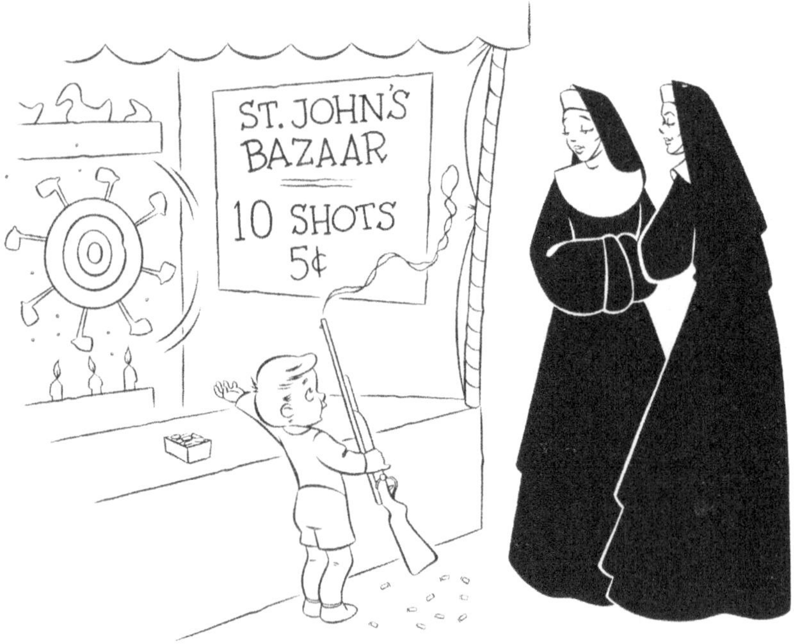
ST. JOHN'S
BAZAAR
10 SHOTS
5¢

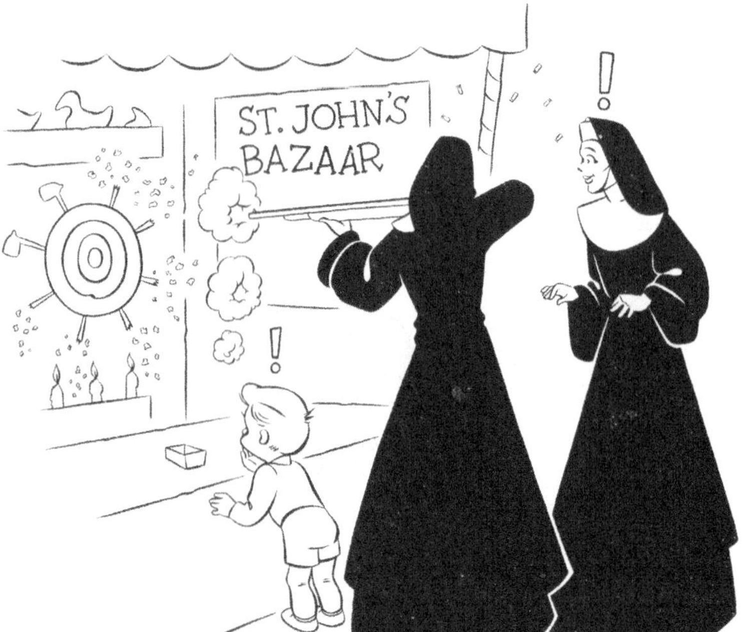
ST. JOHN'S
BAZAAR
!
!

"DUNKING!"

"WHY, MRS. O'LEARY"

"DUCK! THAT WAS MONSIGNOR!"

"NO TIME LIKE THE PRESENT, MR. MIZEY"

"WELL?"

"WHAT CAN YOU LOSE, MONSIGNOR?"

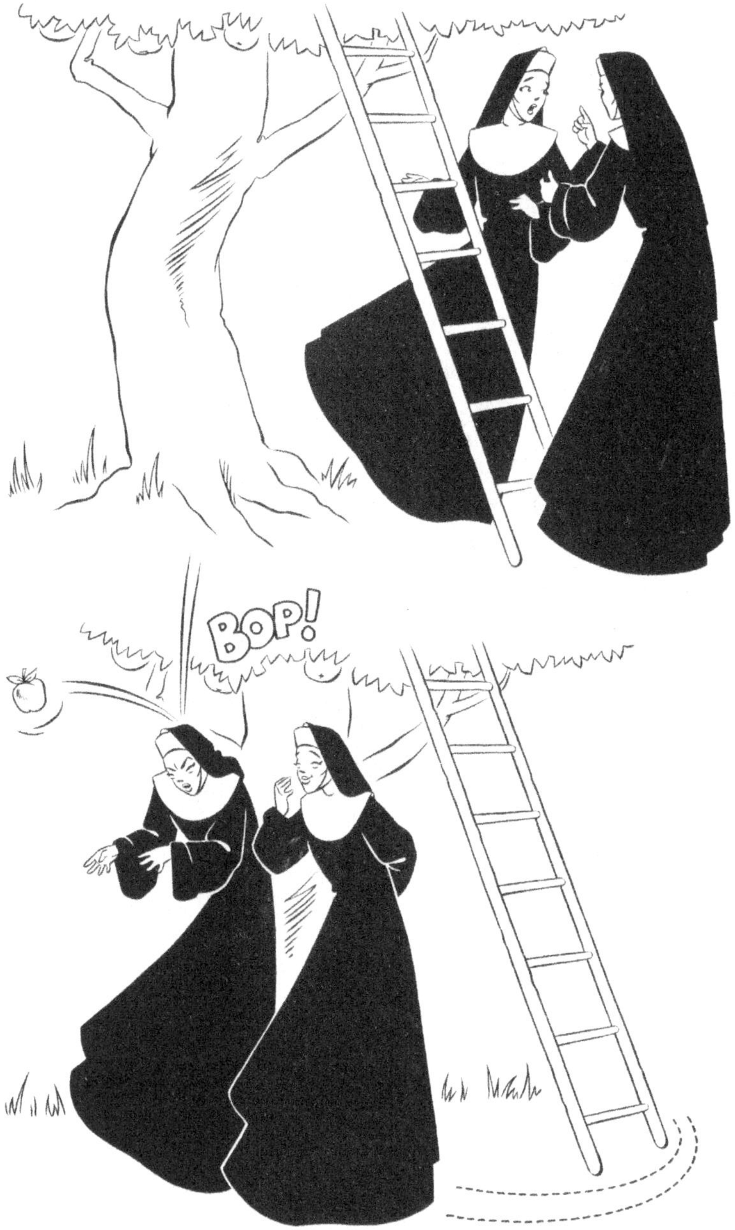
BOP!

"DO YOU THINK ANYONE IS LOOKING?"

"WE BETTER CHANGE THE SHAPE — IT MIGHT OFFEND SOMEONE WE KNOW"

"I HAD HIM IN MY ENGLISH CLASS"

"AIN'T WE LUCKY"

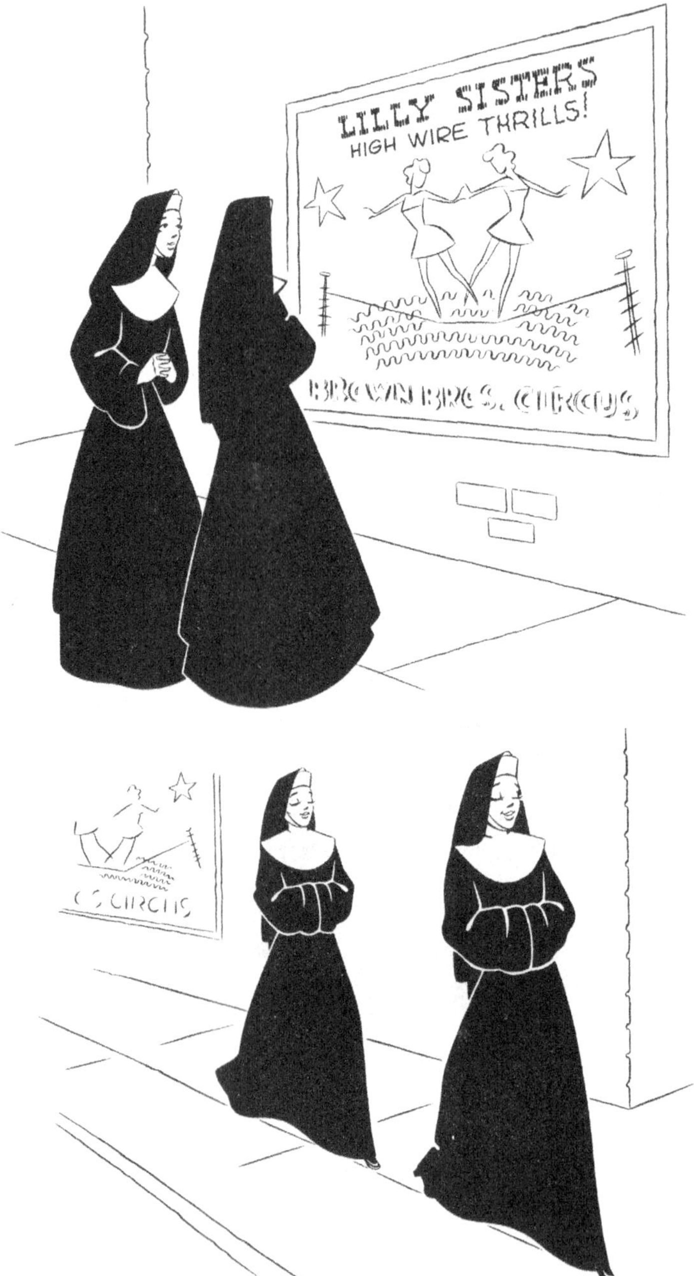
LILLY SISTERS
HIGH WIRE THRILLS!
BROWN BROS. CIRCUS
CIRCUS

"REMEMBER?"

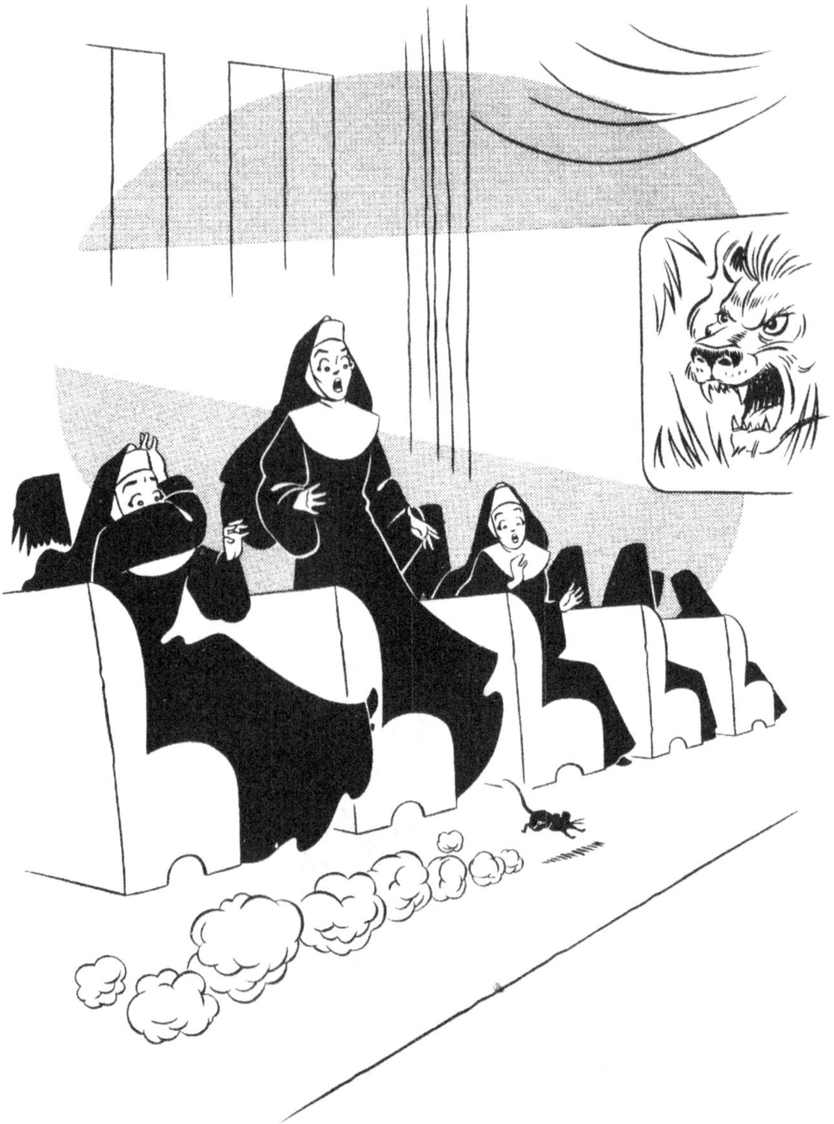

"DUCKY SPOT, ISN'T IT?"

finis

"Psst! Have you seen today's *Daily Nun*??"

A DIFFERENT NUN CARTOON EVERY DAY!

THE DAILY NUN

@DAILYNUN1

ON TWITTER AND INSTAGRAM

DAILYNUN.COM

Classic Catholic Cartoon Collections
FROM ABOUT COMICS

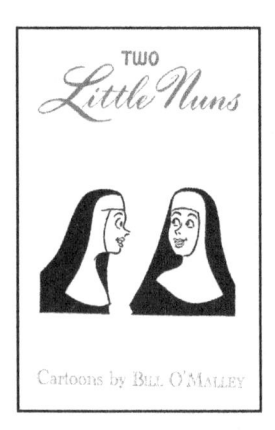

Two Little Nuns — Cartoons by Bill O'Malley

More Little Nuns — Cartoons by Joe Lane

Nuns So Lovable — Cartoons by Joe Lane

Our Little Nuns — Cartoons by Joe Lane

Vale of Dears — Cartoons by Joe Lane

Yes, Sister! No, Sister! — Cartoons by Joe Lane

Look for them where you got this book, or visit **www.AboutComics.com**

Five books worth of nun cartoons in one bargain volume!

Made in the USA
Coppell, TX
11 July 2023